WHAT *is a* TEMPLE?

BY BRIANA KIRKWOOD WRIGHT
ILLUSTRATED BY EMILY BURNETTE

CFI
An Imprint of Cedar Fort, Inc.
Springville, Utah

ISBN 978-1-4621-4748-9

Published by CFI, an imprint of Cedar Fort, Inc.
2373 W. 700 S., Springville, UT 84663
Distributed by Cedar Fort, Inc., www.cedarfort.com

Library of Congress Control Number: 2023952112

Cover and interior layout design by Shawnda T. Craig
Cover design © 2024 Cedar Fort, Inc.
Edited by Jessica B. Ellingson

Printed in the United States of America

10 9 8 7 6 5 4 3 2 1

For my sweet boys,
Anthony and Conrad.
—B. K. W.

To my forever family—
past, present, and future:
you are my heart.
—E. B.

What Is a Temple?

The scriptures teach us the temple is more than a building. It is a special and sacred place we can go to pray, learn, grow our faith, receive blessings, and feel close to God.

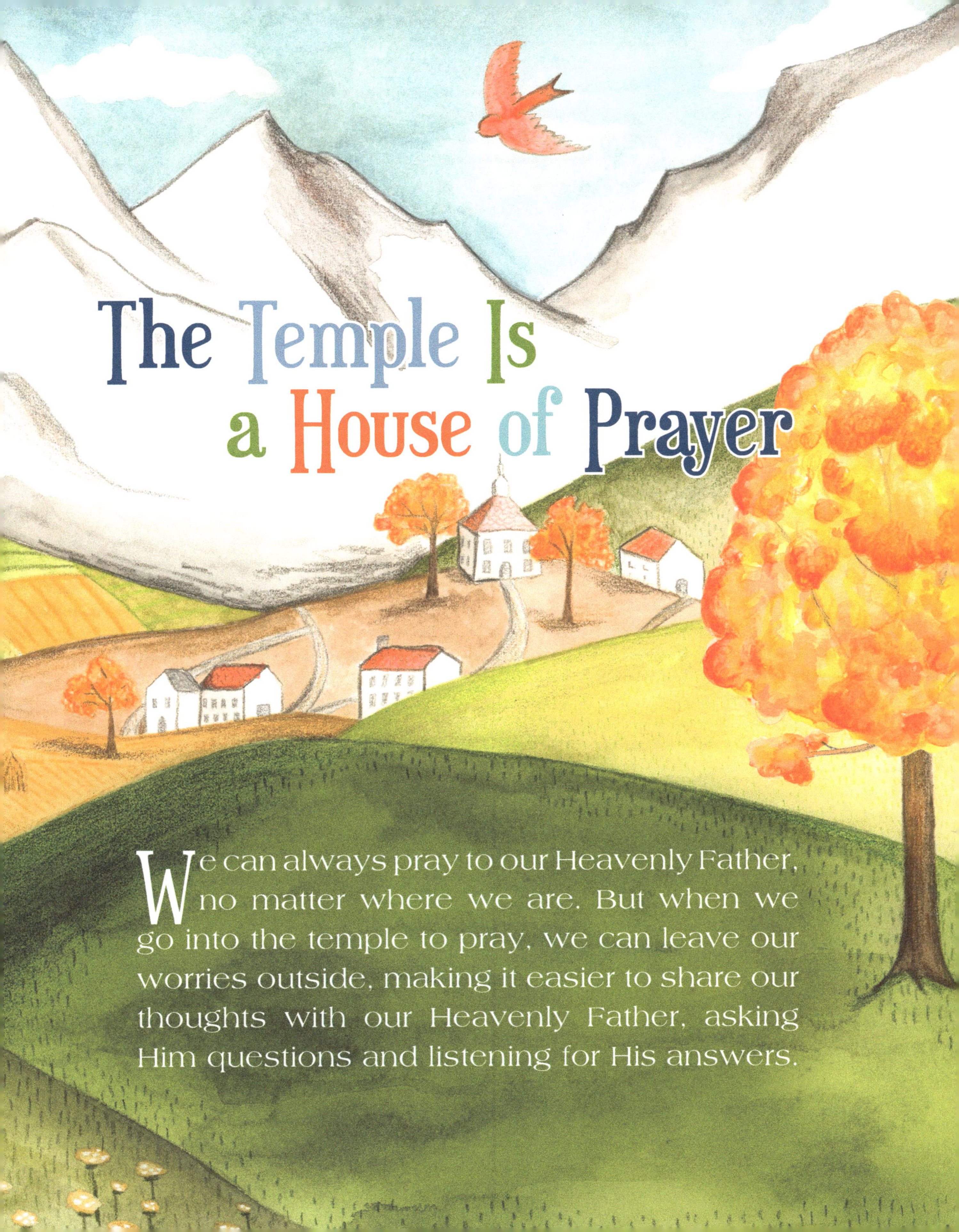

The Temple Is a House of Prayer

We can always pray to our Heavenly Father, no matter where we are. But when we go into the temple to pray, we can leave our worries outside, making it easier to share our thoughts with our Heavenly Father, asking Him questions and listening for His answers.

The Temple Is a House of Fasting

We fast to show the Lord we are willing to sacrifice, or give something up. It reminds us we need to feel the Holy Ghost every day to feed our faith, just like we need food each day to nourish our bodies. Fasting in the temple helps us feel the Holy Ghost.

926

The Temple Is a House of Peace

We can more easily notice the presence of the Holy Ghost because the temple is also a peaceful place. Inside the temple, we try to be quiet and reverent the way we are at church. When we go often, we can learn to recognize how the Holy Ghost speaks to us.

The Temple Is a House of Faith

Faith means to have hope for things we cannot see but believe are real. We know God is real, although we cannot see Him. When we go to the temple, we can show our faith by making covenants with God at special times in our lives, like when we decide to be sealed in the temple!

The Temple Is a House of Promise

Our temple covenants are special promises we make to God, and He blesses us in return. We can also make covenants in the temple for others who did not hear the gospel when they lived on earth. Many people are waiting for your help!

The Temple Is a House of Family

We can be with our families forever! When we are sealed to our family, Heavenly Father promises that even after we die, we will stay together. Inside the temple, husbands and wives can be sealed to each other, and mothers and fathers can be sealed to their children!

The Temple Is a House of Learning

When Jesus was young, He taught the gospel in the temple. He continued to teach in the temple throughout His life. When we go to the temple, we too can learn! We are taught more about Heavenly Father's plan for us and how He can help us live a happy life.

The Temple Is a House of Glory

The temple is a wonderful place to be! It is bright and beautiful to remind us of heaven and our Father who lives there. His glory is that one day we can once again live in His presence with our families. Until then, we can go to the temple to feel close to Him and to each other.

The Temple Is a House of Order

The scriptures tell us everything inside the temple has its place and should be kept neat and clean. To go inside the temple, we must keep ourselves clean as well. We can be worthy to enter by keeping His commandments, like praying, reading our scriptures, and honoring our parents.

The Temple Is a House of God

Do you know what it says on the outside of the temple? By placing His name on the temple, Heavenly Father has shown us it is truly His home: holy and sacred. It is a place on earth set apart from the world where we can come to feel His love.

HOLINESS TO THE LORD • THE HOUSE OF THE LORD

Heavenly Father uses all of these names for the temple so we understand what it means to be in His house. We can make our own home a house of God if we remember the sacred feelings from the temple, try to choose the right, and follow the teachings of Jesus Christ.

What Is the Temple for You?

Here are other words that can be used to talk about the temple. Do you see one that means something special to you? Can you think of other ways going to the temple will bring blessings into your life?

Promise

Healing

GRATITUDE

Joy

Missionary Work

HOPE
Love
FAMILY
Remembering
PEACE

References

What Is a Temple?

"Organize yourselves; prepare every needful thing; and establish a house, even a house of prayer, a house of fasting, a house of faith, a house of learning, a house of glory, a house of order, a house of God" (D&C 88:119; see also 109:8).

Psalm 27:4 | Matthew 10:13
Mark 4:30–32 | D&C 97:16

"I Love to See the Temple," *Children's Songbook*, 95.

The Temple Is a House of Prayer

"Now mine eyes shall be open, and mine ears attent unto the prayer that is made in this place" (2 Chronicles 7:15).

1 Kings 9:3 | 2 Chronicles 6:40
Isaiah 56:7 | Ephesians 6:18
3 Nephi 18:16

The Temple Is a House of Fasting

"For the kingdom of God is not meat and drink; but righteousness, and peace, and joy in the Holy Ghost" (Romans 14:17).

Judges 20:26 | John 14:16–17
D&C 8:2–3

"Bless Our Fast, We Pray," *Hymns*, no. 138.
"Let the Holy Spirit Guide," *Hymns*, no. 143.

The Temple Is a House of Peace

"Enfold me in thy quiet hour / And gently guide my mind / To seek thy will, to know thy ways, / And thy sweet Spirit find" ("Oh, May My Soul Commune with Thee," *Hymns*, no. 123).

Haggai 2:9 | Romans 15:13
Helaman 5:30 | D&C 85:6

"The Holy Ghost," *Children's Songbook*, 105.

The Temple Is a House of Faith

"And now as I said concerning faith—faith is not to have a perfect knowledge of things; therefore if ye have faith ye hope for things which are not seen, which are true" (Alma 32:21).

2 Chronicles 34:30 | Psalm 118:26
James 2:17

"Rejoice, Ye Saints of Latter Days," *Hymns*, 290.

The Temple Is a House of Promise

"And ye were now turned, and had done right in my sight, in proclaiming liberty every man to his neighbour; and ye had made a covenant before me in the house which is called by my name" (Jeremiah 34:15).

2 Kings 23:3 | D&C 128:5
D&C 138:30–37

"Turn Your Hearts," *Hymns*, 291.

The Temple Is a House of Family

"The Prophet Elijah was to plant in the hearts of the children the promises made to their fathers, foreshadowing the great work to be done in the temples of the Lord in the dispensation of the fulness of times, for the redemption of the dead, and the sealing of the children to their parents" (D&C 138:47–48).

Genesis 2:24 — Malachi 4:6
Mosiah 5:15 — D&C 132:46

"Families Can Be Together Forever," *Children's Songbook*, 188.

The Temple Is a House of Learning

"And in the day time he was teaching in the temple; and at night he went out, and abode in the mount that is called the mount of Olives. And all the people came early in the morning to him in the temple, for to hear him" (Luke 21:37–38).

Mark 14:49 — Luke 2:46
Luke 19:47 — Luke 20:1
John 7:14–17 — Mosiah 4:12

The Temple Is a House of Glory

"For behold, this is my work and my glory—to bring to pass the immortality and eternal life of man" (Moses 1:39).

Psalm 26:8 — Isaiah 46:13
D&C 97:15 — D&C 59:1–2

"We Love Thy House, O God" *Hymns*, 247.

The Temple Is a House of Order

"And the Lord said unto me, Son of man, mark well, and behold with thine eyes, and hear with thine ears all that I say unto thee concerning all the ordinances of the house of the Lord, and all the laws thereof; and mark well the entering in of the house, with every going forth of the sanctuary" (Ezekiel 44:5).

Exodus 20:6–12 — 2 Chronicles 8:16
Matthew 19:17–19 — John 14:15
1 John 5:3 — D&C 93:20
D&C 110:8 — D&C 132:8

The Temple Is a House of God

"For behold, I have accepted this house, and my name shall be here; and I will manifest myself to my people in mercy in this house" (D&C 110:7).

Genesis 28: 16–17 — Exodus 20:24
1 Kings 5:5 — 1 Chronicles 23:28
2 Chronicles 7:16 — Matthew 23:21
Revelation 7:15

BRIANA KIRKWOOD WRIGHT started writing poetry and short stories as a creative outlet at the age of eight. Later, she followed that passion and studied literatures in English at the University of California, San Diego, graduating with a bachelor of arts degree. A convert to The Church of Jesus Christ of Latter-day Saints, Briana feels *What Is a Temple?* is the result of an impression she received during the October 2013 general conference. She hopes it will help her share a love of the temple with her sons, Anthony and Conrad. Briana currently lives with her family in Foster City, California. Please visit her at www.brianakwright.com.

For EMILY BURNETTE, creating art has always been an essential part of her life. Beginning at an early age, she would sit at a red folding table in her kitchen and paint masterpieces with her two younger sisters while her mom prepared dinner. As she grew older, she spent long summer days exploring the sage hills of the peaceful Wenatchee Valley and drawing for endless hours. Not much has changed. Emily still paints pictures at her own kitchen table and loves to be outdoors amongst her Savior's creations, although now she gets to experience the magic of wooly bear caterpillars and playing in the ocean's waves through the eyes of her two young sons, Michael and Jack. Nature and the innocence of childhood are constant sources of inspiration for Emily's work. As a self-taught artist, she has developed a unique illustrative style, blending colored pencils and watercolors to create heart-happy art. Emily and her incredibly supportive husband, John, live with their two boys in Seattle, Washington. Visit her at www.emilyburnette.blogspot.com.